CONSCIOUS BLITZ

ANURADHA SRIVASTAVA

Contents

Prologue

Terms and Conditions

The Publisher has strived to be as accurate and complete as possible in the creation of this report, notwithstanding the fact that he does not warrant or represent at any time that the contents within are accurate due to the rapidly changing nature of the Internet.

While all attempts have been made to verify information provided in this publication, the Publisher assumes no responsibility for errors, omissions, or contrary interpretation of the subject matter herein. Any perceived slights of specific persons, peoples, or organizations are unintentional.

In practical advice books, like anything else in life, there are no guarantees of income made. Readers are cautioned to reply on their own judgment about their individual circumstances to act accordingly.

This book is not intended for use as a source of legal, business, accounting or financial advice. All readers are advised to seek services of competent professionals in legal, business, accounting and finance fields.

You are encouraged to print this book for easy reading.

Table Of Contents

Foreword
Chapter 1: Understanding The Importance Of Conscious Growth
Chapter 2: Awareness Of Where Am I?

Chapter 3: Understanding The Level Of Shame
Chapter 4: Understanding The Level Of Guilt
Chapter 5: Understanding The Level Of Apathy
Chapter 6: Understanding The Level Of Grief
Chapter 7: Understanding The Level Of Fear
Chapter 8: Understanding The Level Of Desire
Chapter 9: Understanding The Level Of Anger
Chapter 10: Understanding The Level Of Pride
Chapter 11: Understanding The Level Of Courage
Chapter 12: Understanding The Level Of Neutrality
Chapter 13: Understanding The Level Of Willingness
Chapter 14: Understanding The Level Of Acceptance
Chapter 15: Understanding The Level Of Reason
Chapter 16: Understanding The Level Of Love
Chapter 17: Understanding The Level Of Joy
Chapter 18: Understanding The Level Of Peace
Chapter 19: Enlightenment!
Wrapping Up

Foreword

People act the way they act not because of their upbringing, environment, past experiences or temperament.

I'm not saying that these (upbringing, environment, past experiences or temperament) do not play a part in what happens to a person, they are strong influences – no doubt. But their consciousness levels lay the foundation of their personal growth blueprint.

Here's a good example of how it works.

Let's say you're a high powered CEO or executive that is filled with pride. He may be able to command a legion of employees, but in his personal life, he may experience dysfunctional relationships, lack of spiritual fulfillment or even feel a lack of control over events that are beyond his executorial control (not everyone in the world is his employee and he feels a lack of power because he often borrows strength from his position).

On the other hand, you may have a painter that does not make as much money as the CEO... but is filled with reason, purpose,

fulfillment and love. He is very much in love and passionate with his work, his calling, his desire to produce a masterpiece out of his overflowing reservoirs of endless creativity.

The painter is clearly living at a higher level of consciousness compared to the CEO.

Do you get the picture here?

It's not about your rank, position, car, status or role in life. It's not even in what you're doing or having – it is in your BEING.

A higher level of conscious living will allow one to transcend upbringing, environment, past experiences or temperament to become more than what he or she can be without losing touch with who they really are.

Based on Power Vs Force: The Hidden Determinants Of Human Behavior by David R. Hawkins, the focus on this book centers on the levels of consciousness of human growth.

The path of growth is never ending. It is grafted into our very natures that growth is very important.

But your consciousness level will determine why you will want to grow, how much you want to grow and where you are going to find the resources that will facilitate this process (including finding the right people – the who, to achieve your calling).

This book might change your life. Read it with an open mind.

Conscious Blitz
Learn The State Of Your Consciousness And Methods On How To Increase It

Chapter 1:

Understanding The Importance Of Conscious Growth

Synopsis

Are you pursuing a lifestyle of personal development? Is it effective? By understanding this simple truth, your efforts will give you better results in the long run.

This chapter talks about:

- Why personal development in and of itself is not good enough
- Same goals, wrong intentions
- Finding true meaning in your goals
- 'Ends' goals and 'means' goals
- No accidents!

Personal development as a way of life is very important. Start by understanding how you can fine tune your reasons 'why' and how you can live your life effectively by understanding what consciousness levels are all about!

Consciousness Growth As A Way Of Life

Desiring personal growth in and of itself is not enough.

As enthusiastic as a person may be, if one does not align themselves effectively, they are merely building castles on sand or climbing the so called 'ladder of success' that is leaning against the wrong wall.

Are you aware that your goals are the right goals?

Why is it that two people can pursue the very same set of goals but after accomplishing it, not only turn out drastically different from one another... but also use the results they have achieved in different ways.

(A good example of these 2 people – both would master the art of self defense, but one uses it to kill people but another uses it to learn the art of self-discipline and protect others...)

The example above is a good sign that not all pursuits of personal growth are made equal. If a person is not intrinsically aware of the nature of good and evil (morality), lower level appetites (like smoking or lust), purpose driven living and understanding their egos, the quality of their pursuits and the effectiveness of their results are all defined by a person's awareness and consciousness levels.

That is why David R. Hawkins, author of the book – **Power Vs Force: The Hidden Determinants Of Human Behavior** expounds the ideas that it doesn't matter what social status or rank a person has which determines their desires... it is their consciousness levels that determine if one is living on a lower state of ego, power

hungry, lower appetite addictions and desires or one's life filled with joy, love, meaning, fulfillment, purpose and high level thinking.

Another way to put it, 'means' goals usually pale in comparison to 'ends' goals because some ends are generally more worthwhile compared to others.

(A good way to put it, time management and goal setting is pointless if you are a serial killer. These tools will only help you to kill more people faster. You can't change the means if you want to change the ends. You have to think at a different level and hold to a different principle!)

This is where conscious growth comes in. As people become more aware of what they are supposed to do – giving in to meaning and purpose rather than lower level appetites and addictions, their horizons virtually expand and their thinking becomes better.

To make things simple, remember this rule of thumb – no one got to where they are by accident. It is the way of thinking that got them there. If you want to change your destiny or your outcome, start by changing the way you think.

Chapter 2:

Awareness Of Where Am I?

Synopsis

Learning about the state of your consciousness level is one of the most important things that will change the direction, the effectiveness and the results of your personal growth plan.

This chapter talks about:

- Positive and negative consciousness levels
- Negative ones such as Shame, Guilt, Apathy, Grief, Fear, Desire, Anger and Pride
- Positive ones such as Courage, Neutrality, Willingness, Acceptance, Reason, Love, Joy, Peace and Enlightenment
- Where most of the world are functioning at
- Fluctuations in your personal growth
- Situations that might temporarily shift your consciousness state tremendously
- Subtle influences that will also affect your consciousness

Awareness is very important so make that conscious choice what you want to do with your life by first knowing where you are.

The Different Consciousness Levels

According to Hawkins, different people operate at different levels of consciousness and these levels have a direct influence on their behavioral patterns.

The levels are collectively divided into 2 different groups. The negative group consists of:

Shame, Guilt, Apathy, Grief, Fear, Desire, Anger and Pride

The positive group consists of:

Courage, Neutrality, Willingness, Acceptance, Reason, Love, Joy, Peace and Enlightenment

The transition state is a path of linear growth starting from shame and moving up to pride and then courage and beyond. According to Hawkins 85% of the people on earth live below the level of courage.

Most people tend to fluctuate one to two levels up and down at any given time or circumstances as well as mood swings or fatigue.

However, people will always operate at one specific level in general. They will also fall to a certain level when under pressure but their normative state will determine how they live their lives.

Extraordinary circumstances may also temporary increase or decrease one's consciousness level such as a near death experience, completing a motivation seminar (these will temporary bump up the

consciousness levels for a couple of weeks or days) and negative ones such as discovering a cheating spouse, feeling of extreme failure in things that matter or the death of a loved one (will drop tremendously, sometimes for months...)

Understanding your **core** level is very important but once you know your core level, know that it is worthwhile to invest time and energy into moving up to the next consciousness level.

Moving up a notch is the single, most important result anyone can experience in their lives, sometimes even better than willing a million dollars in a lottery (a person with low consciousness may not have the capacity to handle the money but a person with high consciousness may not have it now, but will develop the skills or utilize resources wisely to get more than that!)

It is also important to know that everything around us can affect our consciousness. The music we listen to, the people we hang out with, the things we feed our mind, listening to the news, even the stuff we hang on our walls can have a strong impact!

We will begin our study about the lowest consciousness state a human being can enter into. Then we will slowly work our way up.

Chapter 3:

Understanding The Level Of Shame

Synopsis

Human beings are born with free will. Unfortunately, that free will is largely robbed from a person when they are at the level of shame.

This chapter talks about:

- Why this is the lowest consciousness level

- What people do at this level
- Who often drops here
- How do you get one out of this level
- How to progress to the next level - guilt

Personal development as a way of life is very important. Start by understanding how you can fine tune your reasons 'why' and how you can live your life effectively by understanding what consciousness levels are all about!

Understanding Shame

Shame is the lowest level consciousness for a human being. According to Hawkins, this level is barely above a dead person – almost like a human zombie. A person at this level might even find it hard to perform basic functions because of the emotional burden they are facing.

A form of self-directed hatred and pain, a person at the level of shame is not able to lift his eyes to see a mirror. Suicidal thoughts are lingering in their minds as humiliation is the only predominant emotion found. Living in shame is excruciatingly painful for no human being would desire to inflict physical torture on themselves but emotional torture can be equally destructive.

The constant reminder of the pain traps them in a mental prison that will eat the person up alive if they are not careful. Lonely and reclusive, they often feel that their presence is also a huge burden on others while being a living parasite at the same time. They often wish they were never born.

What Kind Of People Are At The Shame Level?

The sexually abused, criminals of heinous crimes who got caught and facing inescapable exposure from the public eye, people caught in scandals, suicidal people and even serial killers who have numbed themselves to all aspects of societal norms.

These people will also do whatever it takes to remove themselves from the public eye.

Getting Out Of Shame

Only an extreme amount therapy can get a person out of this stage, otherwise they will most likely remain here for the rest of their lives. Identifying the primary source of pain is important because sometimes, the mind and the body can become so numb to the fact that they become used to the pain and know and would not desire anything else out of it.

A lot of patience is needed as well because their mental repetitions of pain can wear another's patience thin. In an example of sexual abuse, even the mere touch from the opposite (or even same in some cases) sex can kick start the mental trigger of pain and the victim will often close up to all forms of counseling.

Some psychologists even recommend hypnosis in order to induce a patient to overcome these traumas at a sub-conscious level. People who drop down here from a higher level are more hopeful if they are shown a glimpse of hope that they can be restored to their former glory. Or at the very least, elevate their consciousness level to **guilt.**

Chapter 4:

Understanding The Level Of Guilt

Synopsis

Have you ever felt that you have done something wrong in your life and you cannot forgive yourself?

This chapter talks about:

- What is guilt about
- The difference between shame and guilt
- What kind of people exist in this level of consciousness
- Steps to get out of this awful state
- Getting them to stop feeling guilty towards apathy

Yes, we've all done nasty things in our lives. But punishing yourself by feeling guilty does not solve the problem. This chapter handles guilt intelligently by reminding ourselves that there is hope for our lives and constantly beating yourself up is not the solution.

"Imagination is everything; it is the preview of life's coming attractions."

Understanding Guilt

To be honest, guilt isn't really that far from shame. What often happens at this level is a person who experiences painful memories like in shame, but are often having feelings of unworthiness and they find that they are unable to forgive themselves for their past transgressions.

The difference from shame is that they do understand the need to get out of their misery but are often held back by huge negative forces.

People who are stuck here may sometimes entertain thoughts of suicide, though not as perpetual as a person in shame.

Poorly taught (or lopsided) religious teachings can also misguide someone to think they are a dirty sinner with no sense of feeling redeemed.

What Kind Of People Are At The Guilt Level?

People who have failed to live up to their parent's expectations, criminals who got caught in crimes that hurt others, partners caught in adultery and people who feel that they do not measure up.

Religious people with a poor understanding of redemption (dark ages type of thinking) will also think that God sees them as a filthy being.

Getting Out Of Guilt

Educating someone to get out of guilt is better than shame because these people understand a little about the light even though they are overwhelmed in the darkness.

With hard work and positive motivation, one may temporary forget their transgressions and progress to doing some meaningful work to elevate themselves back to normal.

Try not to remind them too much of those incidents and they will be able to do fine for awhile. If successful, they will overcome the pain they are facing and numb themselves with **apathy**.

Chapter 5:

Understanding The Level Of Apathy

Synopsis

The homeless, the hopeless... it is not the society or the environment that makes people apathetic – it is people who believes consciously and subconsciously that life and it's static routine of boredom and a lack of a bright future that entraps the soul.

This chapter talks about:

- What the level of apathy is all about
- The difference between guilt and apathy
- What kind of people exist in this level of consciousness

- How to get people to stop feeling apathetic

- Progressing from apathy to grief

Not caring is not the solution. The problem will persist whether you like it or not. Not accepting responsibility is not the solution either – the result will still be thrust upon you whether you take responsibility or not. If you are in apathy or find someone there, it is time to stand up and get out of this!

Understanding Apathy

Now we are progressing out of the pain and torture into the level of apathy. A person in this stage is at a level of hopelessness and despair. It is a stage of 'I couldn't care less' or 'I don't give a **** (insert any fecal related word here)'.

The person here is totally numb to everything that happens around them. They don't feel pain but they feel so numb that life doesn't have anything they can look forward to at all.

Better than guilt, they don't feel anything at all – which is better than one beating themselves up on a daily basis but not good enough to make any forms of good contribution to society.

What Kind Of People Are At The Apathy Level?

Homeless people, people who are extremely poor, people who have 'tried a lot of things' without success and have practically given up on success, a numb wage slave or some in an unemployed and completely hopeless state.

A recession and depression can also send lots of people temporarily (or in some cases permanently) to this level.

Getting Out Of Apathy

One of the most important things about people living in apathy is the company that they keep.

They are mentally lazy to do anything about it and they often hang around other numb individuals who are equally apathetic.

This is bad because they often reinforce each other's weaknesses to the point that they just don't care anymore.

Changing their environment is very important. The first thing they need to do is to change their friends – introduce some positive individuals into their lives to show them the way.

This group of people is not ready to attend motivational seminars yet because they are not aware of any fundamental need of improvement.

The key is to get them to feel something first. They just don't feel anything unlike the people at the **grief** stage.

Chapter 6:

Understanding The Level Of Grief

Synopsis

The sudden feeling strikes you – that you no longer have your loved one by your side. It is both a celebration of a life and a moment of tragedy at the same time. Such are individuals who are at the level of grief (whether they lost someone or not – it is just the feeling!)

This chapter talks about:

- What the level of grief is all about
- The difference between apathy and grief
- What kind of people exist in this level of consciousness
- Encouraging someone out of grief
- Progressing from grief to fear

Life still goes on whether we like it or not. Feeling sad will only compound the sadness because action begets action. Even though the first step is always the hardest, there lies a better future ahead of us even if the grief of today seems overwhelming.

Understanding Grief

At last we're progressing somewhere with feeling! A person at this level actually feels something, that's the good news.

The bad news is, people who remain at this state as their primary level of consciousness will live an un-achieving life of constant regret and remorse.

This is also a state of perpetual sadness and the feeling of losing someone important in their lives. They are depressed constantly but still better than apathy because at least they are not a numb robot anymore.

What Kind Of People Are At The Grief Level?

People who've felt that they've lost a good opportunity or lost a big deal. The people here feel that they are failures in life. Some students drop here once they fail a final exam or an entry exam into their desired college.

This level is also most commonly felt by someone who has experienced death of a loved one.

Getting Out Of Grief

If this is a temporary case of grief such as the loss of a loved one, it can be overcome if they keep themselves busy with work, hanging out with friends, doing some wholesome activities to keep them from reminding themselves of the pain of the deceased.

Unfortunately for the other group – which is people, who are stuck in a permanent state of grief because they either went bankrupt, lost a big financial deal or loss a good opportunity... they need lots of hard work in order to escape the sorrow.

They need to be reminded of the hope of starting over again.

Dwelling in the same environment is destructive. If they can live and absorb the energy of other positive people who have lost it all but came back from the dead, then they will be able to feel hope once again and move up to a higher level of **fear**.

Chapter 7:

Understanding The Level Of Fear

Synopsis

Oh the fear! Yes, fear is but a word, but also a scary word that paralyzes an individual once it takes form in a person's mind. But what is it that people fear of? Is the fear tangible? Sometimes it could even be the fear of fear itself that hits individuals like Medusa's gaze. Oh the horror...

This chapter talks about:

- What the level of fear is all about
- The difference between grief and fear
- What kind of people exist in this level of consciousness
- Overcoming the fear to progress in life
- Progressing from fear to desire

Repent of your fear this instant! According to the bible, the only fear one must have is of God – not even of the devil for that will be giving too much credit to the devil. Even if you do not believe in the bible, it doesn't matter because fear is the force that drives love away. Perfect love casts out all fear and allows us to see the beauty of life enough to make us want to break out of our cocoon of fear.

Understanding Fear

The grief that is overcome is not easy because now the next logical step for people out of grief is fear. They are sick of feeling like a failure but the fear is a compelling force that will hold them back.

Seeing the world as a place which is filled with danger and a lack of safety, they feel paranoid over every little thing.

These people are too afraid to do anything significant! They fear quitting their job and are willing to be abused by their bosses for the rest of their working life. It goes the same in family relationships as well because they don't have the guts to break away.

What Kind Of People Are At The Fear Level?

People who live in a country that rules with fear. If they are stuck in an abusive relationship and they are on the receiving end, they will often live in fear too.

Sometimes, kids who grow up where the parents often tell them that they cannot do anything will become fearful adults afraid of trying anything at all.

Getting Out Of Fear

There's much one can do to get a person out of fear.

For starters, in order to remove their suspicions and defensiveness common among these paranoid folks, one must continually educate the importance of success stories and comfort zones.

Good motivational seminars will provide a good environment for people to achieve breakthroughs is very important.

A good example is the fire walking exercise used in an Anthony Robbins seminar. The hot coals aren't really that hot if you walk over it fast enough. The only thing that prevents you from walking over is your own fear itself.

These fearful individuals must also be taught that past conditioning is not the only thing that will determine their future outcome. The past does not equate the future – we must believe we can change the past and then we'll only breakthrough to get past fear into the level of **desire**.

Chapter 8:

Understanding The Level Of Desire

Synopsis

The 'want' makes us human. As long as you want something badly enough, the human spirit will entice and empower the individual to do whatever it takes to get whatever it wants. Unfortunately, the problem lies not in the desire but rather the object of desire – which often drives men off the cliffs of sanity.

This chapter talks about:

- What the level of desire is all about

- The difference between fear and desire
- What kind of people exist in this level of consciousness
- Breaking destructive desires
- Progressing from desire to anger

If only human beings can want good stuff – to desire utopia and altruistic goals rather than self centered goals. Desire for self is the stronghold of a 'darkworker' – a person whose love is only directed in one direction... back to themselves. It is important to cultivate good desires otherwise one's ruin is eminent.

Understanding Desire

One of the core functionalities of a human is to want something beyond just our basic needs. Therefore, desire is the first step to motivate someone to get something.

The good news about the level of desire is that people feel motivated to get something started.

The bad news is that at the rudimentary level of desire, it can often lead people into a state of enslavement or addiction to their lower level appetites like smoking, drinking, sex, money, power, prestige, drugs or any other substance that can be abused.

What Kind Of People Are At The Desire Level?

People who lust after something else.

At this level of craving, it can be found in anyone who craves for approval from bosses, peers or parents.

Many other smokers, alcoholics, drug addicts, sex addicts and people who desire with an obsessive behavior are people who are fixated at the level of desire.

Getting Out Of Desire

Consumerism and materialism are the bane of a utopian society. When the society is not taught otherwise, people will fall into lower level materialism and forget the big picture that we are all human beings who live in oneness and not apart from one another.

By instilling good values in a human being, they can be educated in order to help them to overcome.

Additionally, rehab is very important for people who are positive minded and driven, but has one or more lower level desires (e.g. smoking) that will constantly drag them back to the lower states of consciousness.

This is often a psychological effect because under pressure, they tend to fall back on these 'things' to comfort and soothe their pain – which is disguised as a psychological crutch but is a poison that prevents them from becoming the best that they are meant to be.

A person with unmet desires often leads to **anger**.

Chapter 9:

Understanding The Level Of Anger

Synopsis

"Don't make me angry! You Won't Like Me When I'm Angry!"

– The Hulk

This chapter talks about:

- What the level of anger is all about
- The difference between desire and anger
- What kind of people exist in this level of consciousness
- How to get people to stop feeling angry about everything
- Progressing from anger to pride

Don't we all act like the Hulk sometimes? It is not our skin that turns green but rather the mind and the emotions that goes into a haze – which is followed by bitter regret. Anger is more than just an emotion, it is a state of unfulfilled needs and if unattended to, will release the inner hulk in all of us no matter how cordial one appears on the surface.

Understanding Anger

Fear, anger and desire are close cousins of one another. When one is at fear, they want something but they are afraid to get it. But once they overcome the fear, they can remain stuck at desire if they are too comfortable with their addictions.

However, when their desires are often unmet, they enter the level of anger because their desires are not met at a lower level.

This can be a good thing because anger can be a good motivational jumpstart for a lot of people at the lower levels (hey, it is better than nothing which is apathy...) or they can be stuck in this level of hatred for a long, long time.

What Kind Of People Are At The Anger Level?

Similar like people in an abusive relationship, these people are often the abuser rather than the abused. You will constantly see a fear person and an anger person paired together in an inseparable deadlock of vicious abusive cycles.

People who've experienced failure in careers or financial opportunities may often lash out against the world in their fits of rage because they fail to satisfy their lower level desires.

Getting Out Of Anger

The good news about some people in the anger level is that they can get so angry about their lives that they will do whatever it takes to get themselves out of it.

A good example is a person who is so frustrated with his job or his boss that he goes out and starts his own business.

Another example is a child who keeps on wanting to prove to his parents that they can do it or succeed.

Anger people are fairly self motivated and once they accomplish it, they progress (but are often stuck) at the level of **pride**.

Effective teachings and ethical standards must be taught to a person in anger; otherwise, they will wind up causing more harm than good because of their unpredictable or all-or-nothing kamikaze attitude.

Chapter 10:

Understanding The Level Of Pride

Synopsis

Humility is often such a strange word. Someone who strives to be humble will often hit the obstacle of being proud that they are the most humble person in the world – and hence, lose their humility altogether. An oxymoron indeed...

This chapter talks about:

- What the level of anger is all about
- The difference between desire and anger
- What kind of people exist in this level of consciousness
- How to get people to stop feeling angry about everything

- Progressing from anger to pride

They say that pride goes before a fall. How often must one hit into a brick wall so many times before they realize that they are in pain? Yet one cannot inform another of a state of pride until it is too late. Once the walls of pride come down, man learns from their mistakes until they forget their place and the vicious cycle repeats itself.

Understanding Pride

At the highest rung of the negative levels of consciousness, pride is the beginning where a person starts to feel good about themselves. They actually accomplish a lot in their lives and can be really productive to society.

Unfortunately, according to Hawkins, since the majority of people live their lives below this point, this is one level that most people aspire to but their ladder of success is actually leaning against the wrong wall.

This illusion is a false sense of positivity because it is dependent on external or superficial circumstances such as wealth, fame, power, rank, position or things that can easily be taken away.

What Kind Of People Are At The Pride Level?

Some celebrities are at this level because it is all external.

Other people who are at this level are people who are overtly racist, nationalistic, patriotic or fanatical about religion.

Yes, religious fundamentalism is also at this level because of their irrational denial and defensiveness – people are so immersed in their beliefs that they will always see an attack on their beliefs as a personal attack on themselves.

Getting Out Of Pride

It may seem strange to consider it this way, but for most people in the world, pride the highest place a person will ever reach.

The sad thing is that they are not fundamentally aware that the lower levels of consciousness are all that they are taught and they do not know how to transcend beyond it unless their eyes are open.

Sometimes, when they are stripped off their pride and they fall back into the lower levels that they experience a huge paradigm shift that spurs them to seek for something BEYOND pride.

A good example is a person who achieved success in his career and has lots of money but got into an accident or lost someone very important in their lives. They will start to re-think about their purpose here on earth.

Something big must happen to one's life before they can break out of this negative ceiling and finally have hope as they move up to the most critical stage of **courage**.

Chapter 11:

Understanding The Level Of Courage

Synopsis

"Wait a minute... there's something wrong about the way my life is working out! I must seek the solution" – conversations of an awaken man...

This chapter talks about:

- What the level of courage is all about
- Why courage is the doorway to true strength success
- What kind of people exist in this level of consciousness
- Growing from a position of courage
- Getting out of the negativity once and for all!

Congratulations! You realize that there is something wrong with the world – it is time to take the 'Red Pill' of courage or take the 'Blue Pill' of pride and go back to 'sleep' forgetting about your awakening in personal growth. Your life is in your hands – it may be a painful journey because your personal development muscles have atrophied from never using them all your life, but it is worth the struggle – you are now 'the one'... the only one that chooses to change your life.

Understanding Courage

Congratulations! If you are aware of yourself starting at this level,

know that you've made tremendous breakthroughs just to get started at this level.

Courage is the doorway to unlock a life of true meaning and strong personal growth. This level of empowerment us where you stop sucking energy from people around you and you stop getting shifted about by the wind of negativity.

You begin to realize that you are the captain of your own ship and you are totally in charge of your own growth and success in life.

The major difference of one's life as a human being compared to animals is the intrinsic knowledge that the difference between stimulus (external factors) and your response – the ability to recognize the **choice** and make it for the greater good.

What Kind Of People Are At The Courage Level?

People who have awakened to the realization that personal growth is very important to them.

The very people who see life as exciting and challenging instead of feeling overwhelmed by fear or their lower level desires, they want to make a positive change. The point is, they want to be better than they were yesterday so they press on forward.

A student who wants to get good grades because he or she feels good about him or herself is a very good example because they feel that getting good grades in and of itself is already a reward.

Getting Beyond Courage

The inkling of personal growth is already instilled in this person. At this point in time, they might or might not call it personal growth but rather skill-building, career advancement, further education or even life improvement.

The only drawback is that people in the courage level have not had any huge substantial evidence or success in their lives and they need to build up their 'portfolio' of success and progression.

They are willing, but not yet effective or powerful. Attending as many courses, seminars and training is a very good start because this framework gives the courageous people a stepping stone in order to enter into the state of **neutrality**. The growth is just the beginning as they start to awaken to their true purpose.

Chapter 12:

Understanding The Level Of Neutrality

Synopsis

"When you were young and your heart was an open book "You used to say live and let live

"(you know you did, you know you did you know you did)

"But in this ever changing world in which we live in

"Makes you give in and cry

"Say live and let die!"

- Paul McCartney "Live and let die" This chapter talks about:

- What the level of neutrality is all about
- Pros and cons of neutrality
- What kind of people exist in this level of consciousness
- Escaping the complacency
- Moving up from neutrality to willingness

Don't sit by and watch the world die... You are a part of the world – if we don't live together, we'll die alone.

Understanding Neutrality

Welcome to being average. It may surprise you to know that as human beings, most people do not even get out of the negative zone. If the consciousness levels were given a negative to positive scale, neutrality would be at the zero point.

I'm not saying that courage is 'bad', it is just rather the awakening of the consciousness level to leave the negativity behind. Courage is the gateway to success but the forces of negativity are still present.

Neutrality is the state of flexibility. Because people at neutrality are unattached to the outcomes of life, they are extremely satisfied with their level of living. They might not have strong inclinations to 'change the world' or 'change *their* world', but they are doing really fine, they are really okay!

In other words, their mantra in life is, "Live and let live." They are so comfortable with everything that they tend to roll with the punches no matter what happens.

This happens to a lot of people who are in business for themselves.

They play it safe and are doing well but they just don't make the sacrifices necessary because they don't see the need to push themselves.

What Kind Of People Are At The Neutrality Level?

Most of the self-employed, talented but lazy people, the complacent and even the people who've 'made it' in life but don't really get beyond.

In other words, they are epitomized by the phrase, "Good, but not the best".

Getting Beyond Neutrality

It is said that the greatest enemy to get the 'best' is often the good. One can be tied up with seemingly 'good projects' but miss the mark from living their full potential.

A person at the stage of neutrality needs to be given a bigger vision, a bigger understanding of the wholeness of life and living to their true purpose – to fulfill their destiny.

These people are not to be confused with those at the level of pride because prideful living is bad but neutrality is okay but mediocre. In order to incite one's dream to strive beyond neutrality, hanging out with a lot of high conscious, positive, motivating people with huge dreams will give them the **willingness** to embrace their destiny.

Chapter 13:

Understanding The Level Of Willingness

Synopsis

"Don't wait until everything is just right. It will never be perfect. There will always be challenges, obstacles and less than perfect conditions. So what. Get started now. With each step you take, you will grow stronger and stronger, more and more skilled, more and more self-confident and more and more successful."

- Mark Victor Hansen This chapter talks about:
    - What the level of willingness is all about
    - Why willingness supplies the backbone of a successful person
    - What kind of people exist in this level of consciousness
    - How to progress from here
    - Getting from willingness to acceptance

You don't want to be stuck in neutrality – you don't build true strength until you start to push yourself. Don't ever stop growing. If one chooses to stay the same, they will shrink by default because the world is constantly growing.

Understanding Willingness

Welcome to the land of perpetual optimism. At this level, people are aware that they can do anything they want in life. Take can take life by the hands and create unlimited possibilities. Unlike the people at neutrality, just getting by isn't good enough for them anymore.

Instead of being merely 'good', they strive to be the best!

When they have a task at hand, they will do whatever it takes to accomplish it, and accomplish it well! This is the level where the willing person takes what they have and works on their self-discipline, channels willpower to finish the job and does whatever it takes to succeed.

What Kind Of People Are At The Willingness Level?

People who are already safe and comfortable who want to focus on using their energies and talents more effectively.

They no longer want to just get by; they want to do a good, even great job which were not that important when they were in a neutral state. These people form the backbone of a productive society and are the basic 'soldiers' or 'troopers' who will accomplish their mission.

Soldiers who fight well for their country are at this level as are good students who take their studies seriously and strive for excellence. A businessman who has already made enough money (and is no longer working **for** money) is more concerned about excellence and

bringing value to society is also at the level of willingness. As a result, money comes even easier and more to such an entrepreneur!

Getting Beyond Willingness

The biggest challenge about a person to progress beyond willingness is the ability to be effective at everything they are doing. Let's take a sportsman for example. If they are at the level of courage, they are

just getting started – reading books about health, enrolling into a gym, finding good food to eat...

At the neutrality stage, they have good results but they are not pushing themselves to the greatest of their limits. A sportsman at willingness not only pushes their limit, but employs self-discipline, will power, organization skills and is willing to break their boundaries for excellence.

To get past willingness into **acceptance**, a structured life must be in place. They cannot life erratically because without the structure of discipline and organization, it cannot be done. It is important to have a routine that becomes autopilot in one's life. You have to make personal growth your comfort zone. Yes getting out of a comfort zone is important, but you cannot live a life of extremity because willpower can only get you so far.

Chapter 14:

Understanding The Level Of Acceptance

Synopsis

Acceptance – what is there to accept? Only one thing if nothing else... to accept your true calling in your life and to live your life as authentic as possible for what you are called to.

This chapter talks about:

- What the level of acceptance is all about
- Why acceptance is the key to effective goal setting
- What kind of people exist in this level of consciousness
- Growing beyond acceptance
- Progressing to the level of reason

The things at the lower level will no longer hold you back as your desires are geared towards what is most important in your life. Never hold back for you only live once and then, life – life the grass in the field is blown away and gone forever...

Understanding Acceptance

Once you've conquered discipline and organization, then you enter into what is called the level of acceptance.

Courage is the awakening – the realization that you are the source, the originator of good life experiences. But only at the level of acceptance does one effectively create the best experiences.

The things you have learned in the willingness state is extremely crucial because you now have the effectiveness, skills, habits and structure to do great things.

Goal setting and achievement is common at the level of acceptance as one 'accepts' their calling and lives to accomplish it. Not only do you accept responsibility for the world, you accept your destiny to change every area of your life that isn't working (career, health, relationships, bad habits...) You see the big picture now!

What Kind Of People Are At The Acceptance Level?

Disciplined and organized people who want to do the best job in the world. They are people living with purpose, strong goals, powerful motivation and righteous politicians and activists who want to change the world for the better.

Getting Beyond Acceptance

If you want to transcend beyond the level of acceptance, you have to be aggressive in self-improvement.

You can't let any low level desires and addictions hold you back or else you cannot progress.

You have to be able to switch careers to the ones that will help you towards your main goal and not just work for money at the expense of your principles and values.

If you have a health or weight problem, you must solve it through rigorous exercise or changing diets so they won't hold you back.

Very few people at this level are employed because an environment of employment is also filled with lower consciousness people working for a boss with a higher consciousness. A powerful shift must happen before they move into the consciousness of **reason**.

Chapter 15:

Understanding The Level Of Reason

Synopsis

"The important thing is not to stop questioning. Curiosity has its own reason for existing." – Albert Einstein

This chapter talks about:

- What the level of reason is all about
- Why reason is extremely powerful
- What kind of people exist in this level of consciousness
- The only drawback of reason
- Progressing to the level of love

If you are at the level of reason, you will start to document every aspect of your life like a hypothesis. You will become a walking Socrates...

Understanding Reason

Hawkins describes this level as the level of science, medicine, and a strong desire or thirst for knowledge.

Anything that you are doing in this level that isn't brining you towards your greatest goal in life will be eradicated from your life because that is not what you want anymore.

What is important here is that life experiences itself is the proof, hypothesis and theories of high self-conscious growth. You recognize that you are capable of changing the world with your talents and abilities and you start looking around the world to find meaningful contributions to society.

A high level of altruistic thinking plus the intelligence, structure and a sense of calling will elevate people to this level even though few get here their entire lives.

What Kind Of People Are At The Reason Level?

People at this level are people who are high level creators like highly successful engineers, doctors, scientists, architects, researchers and spiritual leaders.

At the very high end, Einstein and Sigmund Freud are at this level

and their hypothesis and studies benefit humanity on a very high level.

Getting Beyond Reason

A person at the level of reason is a walking Socrates. The only drawback of being in this level of reason is that they are unable to separate the subjectivity of the study from the objectivity.

In other words, they miss out on the entire forest because they focus too much on the research on the trees. Their tunnel vision often becomes a stumbling block in their lives because they can't progress further from their levels of consciousness.

Progressing beyond reason is not impossible, though.

When you truly start applying yourself for the good of mankind will you be able to progress beyond reason into the level of **love**.

Chapter 16:

Understanding The Level Of Love

Synopsis

"Love can touch us one time and last for a lifetime and never let go till we're gone."

- Celine Dion "My Heart Will Go On" This chapter talks about:

    - What the level of love is all about

- Unconditional love overflowing
- What kind of people exist in this level of consciousness
- Sharing the love
- Progressing to the level of Joy

Everything seems better when looked through the eyes of love. That unshakable, undeniable feeling that human beings, made in the image of God is what we feel by default. It is no surprise – God is love...

"To live your greatest life, you must first become a leader within yourself. Take charge of your life, begin attracting and manifesting all that you desire in life."

Understanding Love

The level of love is a truly powerful experience. Serving as the guiding light for the greater good of mankind, you allow your heart to be your dominant force rather than your mind.

Living by intuition, your practice of selfless love coupled with the reason of serving humanity, the acceptance of your role on earth to be proactive and the skills and discipline you've developed at the willingness level, you have no other desire except the welfare of the people around you.

What Kind Of People Are At The Love Level?

Mother Theresa and Gandhi.

It is very clear that very few people ever get here in their lives. Hawkins claim that only 1 out of 250 people (or approximately 0.4% of the entire world) ever gets here during their entire lifetimes.

Getting Beyond Love

A very high level thinking – high accomplishment will lead to unspeakable **joy**.

Chapter 17:

Understanding The Level Of Joy

Synopsis

"Joy is a net of love by which you can catch souls." – Mother Theresa This chapter talks about:

- What the level of joy is all about
- Saint-like joy...
- What kind of people exist in this level of consciousness
- Sharing the joy

- Progressing to the level of peace

Love is the true stepping stone to true joy. Once one is filled with so much love, the joy within overflows and doesn't stop. Suppose you realize the joy of being alive, it in and of itself is a fact of unspeakable joy because you have the gift of life.

Understanding Joy

According to Eckhart Tolle – author of the book 'The Power Of Now", this is a state of unspeakable and unshakable happiness. A person at this level of consciousness is extremely powerful. As love becomes more and more unconditional, happiness naturally flows.

Goals and detailed plans is nothing to these individuals because every moment of their lives, they are living according to their purpose and calling since they are already living at a high level.

What Kind Of People Are At The Joy Level?

Advanced spiritual leaders are at this level. A level of sainthood. Nothing can shake joyful people out from this level, even personal tragedy! Everyone who meets with these people is inspired.

A person who experienced a near-death experience can also temporarily shoot up to this level.

Getting Beyond Joy

True joy is experienced by very few. That is why it is impossible to teach another how to get beyond joy. The next stage is **peace.**

Chapter 18:

Understanding The Level Of Peace

Synopsis

Peace, when all is still... for one who has truly seen or experienced their creator in their lives (not necessarily through personal

revelation but rather through what God has done...) This chapter talks about:

- What the level of peace is all about
- What kind of people exist in this level of consciousness
- What lies beyond the state of peace

No more does life matter when one is at the level of peace. It is almost as though the individual and God become one.

Understanding Peace

The day one lives their lives in complete and utter surrender to their creator, you've reached the place where Hawkins describe as

'illumination'.

Everything is still before God. The mind is silenced to a point of undeniable peace. Impossibly able for anyone to fathom, this level is only reached by 1 in 10 million people!

What Kind Of People Are At The Peace Level?

Ultra spiritual people who've reached their true calling, has inexhaustible reservoirs of love, joyful beyond measure and peaceful before an almighty God are at the levels of peace.

Getting Beyond Peace

It is humanly impossible to get beyond peace to **transcendence**.

Chapter 19:

Enlightenment!

Synopsis

"I pray also that the eyes of your heart may be enlightened in order that you may know the hope to which he has called you, the riches of his glorious inheritance in the saints, and his incomparably great power for us who believe." (Ephesians 1:18 – the bible)

This chapter talks about:

- What the level of enlightenment is all about
- What kinds of people exist in this level of consciousness if any...?
- The highest ever!

It is almost impossible to contemplate what goes on up here. Maybe one who has truly seen God face to face can achieve enlightenment. It's possible but really few. One who gets here is truly one in a million.

Understanding Enlightenment

This stage is the highest possible attainment of human consciousness

- it is almost God-like.

What Kind Of People Are At The Level Of Enlightenment?

Jesus Christ, Buddha, Krishna are here. Even people think about these individuals, their own consciousness levels are raised up in the process.

Wrapping Up

A path of growth is never ending. Progress makes life worth living. If you have grown in the consciousness scale, you will definitely appreciate the growth you have gone through when you look back and say "Ah, here I was last year in the stage of pride..." The reflection is truly enlightening.

Remember to identify your overall level. Attending a motivational seminar will temporarily bump you up the consciousness scale. Try and recognize what brings it up and what brings it down.

Do not try and short cut the process. Each level is a foundation to another (unless you are talking about the negative ones – please just skip straight to courage!) Also recognize where you are under pressure. Don't beat yourself up if you can't be at a certain stage because going up one level is extremely hard!

Don't stop growing...

Printed by Libri Plureos GmbH in Hamburg,
Germany